Robin Prince Monroe

DEVOTIONS
FOR THE
BROKENHEARTED
HOPE FOR THE GRIEVING

To Barb,
Thank you for
your encouragement
and prayers.
Finally!

TATE PUBLISHING, LLC

ISBN: 1–5988635–2-5

To my husband, Merlin,
who patiently loved me
through all the pain.
I love you with all my heart.

The Lord is close to the brokenhearted
and saves those who are crushed in spirit.

—Psalm 34:18

Table of Contents
Loss of a Loved One

Moving On

Author's Note

This book, originally published in 1994, had quite a long title, *In This Very Hour, Devotions for Your Time of Need: Loss of a Loved One.* After the publisher sold almost every copy it had on hand the book went out-of-print in 1999. Since then I have received numerous letters and e-mails from people all over the country looking for it. I have given all but my own copy out to families who needed the comfort that God had graciously allowed me to be a part of. Except for the "Moving On" sections and a few minor edits the following is exactly as I first wrote it during what was for me still an intense time of pain. It is with much love and many prayers that it is made again available to you.

Acknowledgments

Special thanks to Nancy Koesy Parker, a very talented writer and editor, my dear friend and writing buddy. She read, edited, groaned, prayed and cheered for me through the first publication of these devotions in 1994, and in spite of the wisdom she acquired over the past eleven years she reread, re-edited, groaned, prayed and cheered for me through the preparation of this new edition.

And to Pam McAlister, who walked with me through my darkest valleys, held me up when I was unable to stand, continues to be there for me no matter what new challenges come my way, and makes me laugh so hard my stomach aches.

I know God sent you both to me because He knew I couldn't make it without you. I love you deeply and thank Him for you every day.

Preface

God laid it on my heart to write most of this book two years after our daughter died. After Anna's death, my heart was broken and I sought comfort the only place I knew to search—in God's Word. The passages that Christians often quote in difficult times, like Romans 8:28, didn't help me then. But our Lord didn't let me down. Other Scripture began to take on new meaning. My prayer is that you will find here some small amount of comfort during your time of grieving.

Most devotions are written to be read daily, but during your time of struggle you may need to read only one a week or even one a month. Be gentle with yourself. Like a tiny child, let your strong Father take you by the hand and tenderly lead you through the raging storm. Even if you try to let go of Him, He won't let go of you.

... Because God has said,
"Never will I leave you;
never will I forsake you."
So we say with confidence,
"The Lord is my helper; I will not be afraid ... "
Hebrews 13:5–6

Prologue

Our Story

Our son Daniel was born August 16, 1985. We were so excited and thankful for this much awaited addition to our happy family. Big brother Caleb and big sister Anna held the newborn when he was only a few hours old.

But we soon realized something was wrong. Daniel wouldn't nurse at all. The next day the doctor came in, and told me as gently as possible that Daniel had symptoms of Down's syndrome. He said he could test him now or wait until he was a little bigger. We chose to wait, not for one moment believing it could be true.

Four months later, in December, Daniel was put in the hospital with bronchitis. While he was there, they drew blood and sent it to the genetic center. Because of the holidays the answer was delayed. It wasn't until January that we found out Daniel did have Down's. We began to grieve—to grieve over the little boy we thought we had, the normal little boy that would read a book, grow up, and have a family. And we began to accept the precious gift God gave us instead.

Daniel was in the hospital eight times over the next three years with respiratory problems, mostly pneumonia. He slept only three or four hours a night. Our son Caleb also went into the hospital during that time to have his appendix out. My husband, Merlin, was working third shift so he wasn't home at night to help me with the children, but he would often forego his sleep in the daytime so I could nap.

Shortly after Daniel was diagnosed with Down's, he began to have seizures (myoclonic jerks), sometimes fifty a day. When he was put on medication to control them, he stopped smiling. It was two years before we saw him smile again.

Aware that this time was as difficult for our other children as for us, Merlin and I tried to spend time alone with each of them. We would have special dinners out or let them help with the grocery shopping. Many times Anna and I would have a picnic lunch in the front yard while Daniel napped.

During the summer of 1987, we took Caleb and Anna to Disney World. More than anything Anna wanted to see Minnie Mouse. She kept asking me, "Where is Minnie Mouse, Mommy?" Just as we were leaving the park Minnie came out for autographs and Anna got to shake her hand. It was a special time for all of us.

One day, almost in tears, Anna asked me, "Mommy, why does Daniel have seizures?" I explained that Daniel's brain didn't work right. She said, "No, I mean why doesn't God fix them?" I told her, "I don't know, sweetheart, but God loves us and we have to believe that He knows what is best for us." With a little girl's certainty, she responded, "Well, when I get to heaven I'm gonna talk to God about that."

That August Anna started first grade. She was proud to be at the big school with her brother, Caleb. In September, she had her physical—"healthy" was written on the doctor's form.

Then on October 2, Anna complained about feeling bad. She had a small bruise on her leg and said it hurt a lot. She had a low-grade fever, so we decided she must have a virus. Over the weekend, she felt worse, so we called the doctor. He also thought it could be a virus, but he asked us to bring her in on Monday.

At the doctor's office Monday afternoon, we noticed how carefully he checked her over, so much that we commented on it on the way out. We took comfort in his promise that if she didn't get better by Friday, he would order some blood work.

But that evening, she began to feel worse, and around 11:00, she threw up blood. Even though she had seen the doctor that day, I knew something terrible had to be wrong. I called Merlin at work and told him to come home quickly and asked him to call a friend of ours to come and stay with the boys. Then I called the doctor.

While I was waiting for the doctor to return my call, I lay with Anna in her bed. She cried, "Mommy, Mommy, pray for me!" So we prayed that Jesus would come and help her.

The phone rang and I ran to answer it. It was the doctor. He said that I should take her to the hospital; he would meet us there. When I returned to Anna's room she was smiling. She said, "Mommy, thank Him!" When

I asked, "Who, darling?" she answered, "Jesus—Jesus is here helping me." She wasn't conscious after that.

Merlin came home and we rushed her to the hospital. By the time we got there, I could see small spots of blood under the skin on her gums. Our doctor had her blood tested right away. He came in and told us that our precious daughter had leukemia.

I remember saying, "I can't do this!" Merlin left the room to call our families. I felt nauseated. I asked our doctor to pray with me. I couldn't pray; I needed his words. We admitted her, and in the room, I lay beside her once again. The doctor came in to tell us that in the morning a specialist would see Anna so we could decide on treatment. Then Anna had a seizure and they rushed her to intensive care.

The leukemia had caused a hemorrhage in her brain. After they put her on a machine to take the white blood cells out of her blood, then surgery to relieve the pressure from the hemorrhage, Anna died. On October 8, 1987, she went to be with our Lord.

In February 1988, Daniel stopped having seizures. The doctors don't know why. I believe a little girl "talked to God about that."

I

Someone Reaching

But we have this treasure in jars of clay to show that this all-surpassing power is from God and not from us. We are hard pressed on every side, but not crushed; perplexed, but not in despair; persecuted, but not abandoned; struck down, but not destroyed.

—2 Corinthians 4:7–9

After Anna died, when I was asked how I felt, I said, "My heart is broken, my spirit is crushed, and I hurt so bad I want to die." I just wanted to lie down and give up the work of trying to get through each day. When you are grieving it takes a tremendous amount of effort just to get out of bed.

This Scripture came to mind again and again during those first few days. It brought me no feeling of comfort—no feeling of closeness to God. It was just there, like a dangling rope thrown to a drowning man. I couldn't grasp it, but it meant that there was Someone out there trying to reach me.

2

Cry Out

Listen to my cry, for I am in desperate need.

—*Psalm 142:6*

How long, O Lord? Will you forget me forever? How long will you hide your face from me?

—*Psalm 13:1*

Yet I am poor and needy; may the Lord think of me. You are my help and my deliverer; O my God, do not delay.

—*Psalm 40:17*

Cry out to God for help. If you have no words of your own, use these words from Scripture.

3

The Morning After Tears

How I long for the months gone by, for the days when God watched over me, when his lamp shone upon my head and by his light I walked through darkness! Oh, for the days when I was in my prime, when God's intimate friendship blessed my house, when the Almighty was still with me and my children were around me, when my path was drenched with cream and the rock poured out for me streams of olive oil.

—Job 29:2–6

You are so tired, but sleep comes only after tears. You begin to waken; you start to sense the light of morning. You don't want to wake up because you know if you do, you will find out that it all really happened. You long for the mornings when you woke up and life was good, when life was "normal."

4

Christ Your Intercessor

My face is red with weeping, deep shadows ring my eyes; yet my hands have been free of violence and my prayer is pure. O earth, do not cover my blood; may my cry never be laid to rest! Even now my witness is in heaven; my advocate is on high. My intercessor is my friend as my eyes pour out tears to God; on behalf of a man he pleads with God as a man pleads for his friend.
—Job 16:16–21

"As a man pleads for his friend." Christ is your intercessor. He is pleading with God. He is pleading for you, His friend.

5

A Man of Sorrows

He was despised and rejected by men, a
man of sorrows, and familiar with suffering.
Like one from whom men hide their faces he was
despised, and we esteemed him not. Surely he
took up our infirmities and carried our sorrows,
yet we considered him stricken by God, smitten
by him and afflicted. But he was pierced for our
transgressions, he was crushed for our iniquities,
the punishment that brought us peace was upon
him, and by his wounds we are healed.
—Isaiah 53:3–5

"How many children do you have?" should be an easy way to start a conversation. I usually say. "I have three children here and a little girl in heaven." But I can tell you that many times it costs me to answer honestly. People are often uncomfortable. I can almost see them get out their bricks to build a wall. It is not by accident that "rejected by men and familiar with suffering" are in the same sentence here. I am a mother's worst nightmare: I have a profoundly retarded son, and my little girl died. No one wants to be reminded that life can be like that.

But Christ was "a man of sorrows and familiar with suffering." He knows exactly how you feel, and "by his wounds we are healed."

6

It's Okay to Hurt

If you are up to it, read John 11:1–44

When Jesus saw her weeping, and the Jews who had come along with her also weeping, he was deeply moved in spirit and troubled. "Where have you laid him?" he asked. "Come and see, Lord," they replied. Jesus wept. Then the Jews said, "See how he loved him!"

—*John 11:33–36*

Jesus knew that in a very short time He would raise Lazarus from the dead, just as you know that you will see your loved ones in heaven again if they know the Lord. But still, He cried. His friend had died. Death means separation, if only for a time.

"*Jesus* wept." It is not wrong to grieve. Jesus grieved. Go ahead and cry. Cry all you need to cry. Jesus cried. It's okay to hurt. It's all right to cry.

7
You Are Not Alone

I am poured out like water, and all of my bones are out of joint. My heart has turned to wax; it has melted away within me. My strength is dried up like a potsherd, and my tongue sticks to the roof of my mouth; you lay me in the dust of death.

—Psalm 22:14–15

Grieving is physical—and exhausting. I remember feeling stabs of pain in my chest for months after our daughter died. I remember feeling as if I couldn't breathe. It felt like there was a heavy weight on my chest.

People will tell you, "You need to work through this." That is exactly what you are doing. You are working. You are carrying a terribly heavy load. But you are not alone.

8

They Were Not Disappointed

My God, my God, why have you forsaken me? Why are you so far from saving me, so far from the words of my groaning? O my God, I cry out by day, but you do not answer; by night, and am not silent. Yet you are enthroned as the Holy One; you are the praise of Israel. In you our fathers put their trust; they trusted you and you delivered them. They cried to you and were saved; in you they trusted and were not disappointed.
—Psalm 22:1–5

Sometimes the agony is so great that the pain itself separates you from other people. Times like these are difficult, but even more difficult is when you feel separated from God—feeling that He doesn't hear your pleading and screaming. You know in your head that God is there, yet in your heart you feel abandoned. Don't let yourself forget: "They cried to you and were saved, *in you they trusted and were not disappointed.*"

9

Your Hope Is God

Why are you downcast, O my soul? Why are you so disturbed within me? Put your hope in God, for I will yet praise him, my Savior and my God.

—Psalm 43:5

Sometimes you will need to speak to yourself. There will be days you will need to remind yourself that your hope is in God. No matter how you feel, your only hope is in Him.

10

Jesus Didn't Lie

I tell you the truth, you will weep and mourn while the world rejoices. You will grieve, but your grief will turn to joy . . . I have told you these things, so that in me you may have peace. In this world you will have trouble. But take heart! I have overcome the world.

—John 16:20, 33

Somebody lied to me. Somebody told me that my life would be good. I knew I would have little ups and downs, but like the resolving of conflict in a thirty-minute sitcom, I thought the hurt in my life would disappear. Like the coyote in the cartoon, I could crash in a canyon, then pick myself up and walk away unscathed.

Jesus didn't lie. He told me there would be trouble. But I can take heart! He has overcome the world.

I I

Be Gentle with Yourself

> *. . . and had John beheaded in the prison.*
> *His head was brought in on a platter and given*
> *to the girl, who carried it to her mother. John's*
> *disciples came and took his body and buried*
> *it. Then they went and told Jesus. When Jesus*
> *heard what had happened, he withdrew by boat*
> *privately to a solitary place. Hearing of this, the*
> *crowds followed him on foot from the towns.*
> *When Jesus landed and saw large crowd, he had*
> *compassion on them and healed their sick.*
> *—Matthew 14:10–14*

The first thing Jesus did when He heard about John's death was to go off by Himself. He gave in to His sorrow and allowed His heart time to heal. Only later did He respond to the crowd. There will be times when you need to be alone. Give in to those times. There will be times when you want to be with people. Be gentle with yourself.

12

The Fellowship of His Suffering

I want to know Christ and the power of his resurrection and the fellowship of sharing in his sufferings, becoming like him in his death, and so, somehow, to attain to the resurrection from the dead.

—Philippians 3:10

There were times when people would say to me, "God picks special people to be the parents of a handicapped child." I wanted to scream, "I don't want to be special!" And as I wrestled with God I said, "I don't want to understand Christ's pain. I just want His pain and mine to be gone." If you have never really hurt—if you have never really hurt so bad you thought you would die—then Christ's suffering feels completely foreign, utterly unreachable. But if your heart has really been broken, His hurt becomes something you can almost touch. And we can't forget: His terrible pain and glorious resurrection is our invitation to eternal life.

13

God Is Big Enough

I am the man who has seen affliction by the rod of his wrath. He has driven me away and made me walk in darkness rather than light; indeed, he has turned his hand against me again and again, all day long . . . So I say, "My splendor is gone and all that I had hoped from the Lord." I remember my affliction and my wandering, the bitterness and the gall. I will remember them, and my soul is downcast within me.

Yet this I call to mind and therefore I have hope: Because of the Lord's great love we are not consumed, for his compassions never fail. They are new every morning; great is your faithfulness. I say to myself, "The Lord is my portion; therefore I will wait for him."

—Lamentations 3:1–3, 18–24

Well-meaning friends say things trying to make you, and themselves, feel better, things like "God must have needed her more in heaven," or "God didn't let this happen, the evil in the world caused it." Those kinds of statements made me want to punch somebody in the nose or just throw up. And those words were confusing at a time when my relationship with God already felt so confused.

I do not know how the evil and hurt in this world fit in with a loving and good God. No one knows. But God has control over disaster. Had He wanted my daughter to be alive now, she would be. If I don't believe that, then my God is either powerless—unable to help my daughter, even if He wanted to—or His back was turned while it all happened. Understanding that God allowed this tremendous pain made me very angry with Him for a long time. Scripture is clear about who allowed the pain, but it is also very clear about God's love, faithfulness, and compassion.

You may feel angry, but God is big enough to handle your anger. Open your heart to Him.

14
Why?

*Though He slay me, yet will I hope in Him;
I will surely defend my ways to His face. Indeed
this will turn out for my deliverance, for no
godless man would dare come before him.*
—*Job 13:15–16*

Why? Why? Why? The word tears at your mind
and heart like a vicious dog. You try to think of
reasons—*now she won't have to suffer; I can help someone
else who is grieving; these things just happen.* But there is
just no reason or explanation that can quiet the gnawing
pain.

After a time of screaming "Why?" you realize that
even the best reasons or explanations only bring disappointment. God's well-thought-out plan is incompre-
hensible to our human minds. But "though He slay me,
yet will I hope in Him."

15

Is This My Fault?

How many wrongs and sins have I committed? Show me my offense and my sin. Why do you hide your face and consider me your enemy?

—Job 13:23–24

In the land of Uz there lived a man whose name was Job. This man was blameless and upright; he feared God and shunned evil.

—Job 1:1

There must have been a better way for God to accomplish His purpose. So why didn't He find that better way? Then the painful thought grows within me. *Is this my fault? Is it because of my sin? Am I so awful that this was the only way God could get my attention?*

No! Job was "blameless and upright; he feared God and shunned evil." Yet Job had to endure greater trials than I can begin to imagine.

Then why? Only God knows. Was it because of my sin? Most probably not.

16

How Are You?

If I say 'I will forget my complaint, I will change my expression and smile,' I still dread all my sufferings, for I know you will not hold me innocent.

—*Job 9:27–28*

The first time you go back to church can be difficult. Friendly questions like "How are you?" become insurmountable obstacles. Do you smile and say, "I'm okay" or even "I'm fine"? Or do you try to explain the depth of your despair? Do they really want to know how you are?

Some very special people *do* want to know, but many others do not. And you are too emotionally exhausted at this time to try to figure out how to answer them.

Sometimes people need a glimpse of your heart. Just take one person at a time and let God give you the words. Continually hiding your aching heart is not only exhausting, it's a lie.

17

Let Go of the Whys

When I tried to understand all this, it was oppressive to me till I entered the sanctuary of God; then I understood their final destiny.
—Psalm 73:16–17

Trying to understand why is a natural part of the grieving process, but there comes a time when you need to let go. Trying to understand can paralyze you from moving on.

Be assured, the "whys" will come back. But when they do return, they won't be quite as demanding or last quite as long.

18

You Will Laugh Again

Like one who takes away a garment on a cold day, or like vinegar poured on soda, is one who sings songs to a heavy heart.
—*Proverbs 25:20*

There will be times when a cheerful word or a happy song will make you want to cover your ears. I remember a beautiful, sunny day when I was especially down. My heart felt rainy. I needed the hugs and tears of others. Their smiles and cheer only made my pain clearer, sharper.

Times will come when you desperately need to laugh and feel normal. You may wonder if you will ever feel like laughing again. You may even feel guilty if you find yourself having fun. But you will laugh again. The normalcy of life will begin to return—but this time everything will be a little different.

19

Wrestling with God

Jesus went out as usual to the Mount of Olives, and his disciples followed him. On reaching the place, he said to them, "Pray that you will not fall into temptation." He withdrew about a stone's throw beyond them, knelt down and prayed, "Father, if you are willing, take this cup from me; yet not my will, but yours be done." An angel from heaven appeared to him and strengthened him. And being in anguish, he prayed more earnestly, and his sweat was like drops of blood falling to the ground.

When he rose from prayer and went back to the disciples, he found them asleep, exhausted from sorrow. "Why are you sleeping?" he asked them. "Get up and pray so that you will not fall into temptation."

—Luke 22:39–46

More than any other Scripture this passage brings me comfort. Jesus, the perfect Son of God, anguished over the pain He was asked to bear. For some reason, in our society, particularly in Christian circles, we are made to feel guilty if we grieve. "What's wrong? Don't you trust God?" "You should be better by now." This is especially true as time passes. But Jesus—perfect Jesus—anguished. His pain was so great that blood oozed out of his pores. If Jesus could hurt like that, then it must not be sinful when I hurt. He asked God, not once, but three times (Matt. 26:36–46) to take His burden away.

In his anguish, Jesus wrestled with God. Ultimately He accepted God's will, but He *did* wrestle. I, too, wrestled with God. In my sinfulness the wrestling takes longer. But it must be okay to wrestle with God; Jesus did.

20

Not Without Hope

Brothers, we do not want to be ignorant about those who fall asleep, or to grieve like the rest of men, who have no hope. We believe that Jesus died and rose again so we believe that God will bring with Jesus those who have fallen asleep in him. According to the Lord's own word, we tell you that we who are still alive, who are left till the coming of the Lord, will certainly not precede those who have fallen asleep. For the Lord Himself will come down from heaven, with a loud command, with the voice of the archangel and with the trumpet call of God, and the dead in Christ will rise first. After that, we who are still alive and are left will be caught up with them in the clouds to meet the Lord in the air. And so we will be with the Lord forever. Therefore encourage each other with these words.

—1 Thessalonians 4:13–18

Not long after my daughter died, I remember trying to offer some little comfort to my grieving son, Caleb. I told him, "Caleb, we will see Anna again. When we go to heaven she will meet us there and then we will have forever together."

He looked at me with tears in his eyes and said, "But, Mama, that will be a long time from now, maybe seventy years. I wish we could take a rocket and go visit her now."

I knew so very well what he was feeling. We missed her terribly and we knew that we would never again enjoy our beautiful Anna until this life ended. The knowledge that we would see her later, much later in Caleb's eyes, didn't seem to help.

But what if we didn't know even that? What if we believed this was the end and there would never be a chance to see her again? What if we believed that she had just ceased to exist? I can't imagine that kind of hopelessness.

Although you are in terrible pain now, your grief is not like the "rest of men, who have no hope."

21

Fear

*When I am afraid, I will trust in you. In
God, whose word I praise, in God I trust; I will
not be afraid. What can mortal man do to me?*
—*Psalm 56:3–4*

One day a child is giggling and wrestling with her
brother. The next week she is gone. Now when
you look at other people you love, you know how fragile life is. You are filled with fear. Not all the time, but
when you least expect it, fear jumps out like a monster
in ambush.

Your husband is late from work and you picture
him wrecked somewhere. Your son is going to an amuse-
ment park, and you fear he will get lost or be kidnapped.
Your other child is in bed with a raging fever and you
know it must be meningitis.

You have three choices when you are confronted
by these moments of fear: You can try to protect yourself.
You can panic. Or you can trust in God.

You know from past experience that trust does not
mean that everything will turn out the way you think it

should. Trust means that no matter what happens, God is in control and He will stay beside you. It is a moment-by-moment leaning on Him. You will feel fear. But as you pass through those times of fear, you learn to keep coming back to God and the reality that He is good and that He deeply and completely loves you.

22

When God Says No

Father, if you are willing, take this cup from me; yet not my will but Yours be done.
                    —*Luke 22:42*

Ask and it will be given to you, seek and you will find; knock and the door will be opened to you. For everyone who asks receives; he who seeks finds; and to him who knocks, the door will be opened.
        Which of you, if his son asks for bread, will give him a stone? Or if he asks for a fish, will give him a snake? If you, then, though you are evil, know how to give good gifts to your children, how much more will your Father in heaven give good gifts to those who ask Him!
                    —*Matthew 7:7–11*

Anna was in the hospital only a few days before her death. Yet in that time, people all over the United States heard about her illness and prayed for her. So many people were pleading for Anna's life, but God said no.

For reasons only He understands, God chose for Anna to die.

Christ also pleaded with His Father, "Let this cup pass from Me." God said no to His own beloved Son.

Prayer has been difficult these past five years. I have no trouble just talking to God about things as I would a friend, but it is very hard for me to ask Him for anything. There are times when I don't know what to think as I read the above scriptures. I asked for Anna to be healed. It feels like God gave me the snake.

These questions and feelings are still somewhat unresolved in my heart. But I do pray. I pray for others who are ill or in trouble. I pray because God wants me to. I pray out of obedience. I pray because Jesus did even when God said no, and I pray because God is my Father.

Like a small child who wants cake for supper or wants to run in the street, many times I come to God not knowing the eventuation of my requests. But because God does understand, and because He sees the whole picture, sometimes He says no.

23

The Hope of Heaven

All these people were still living by faith when they died. They did not receive the things promised; they only saw them and welcomed them from a distance. And they admitted that they were aliens and strangers on earth. People who say such things show that they are looking for a country of their own. If they had been thinking of the country they had left, they would have had opportunity to return. Instead, they were longing for a better country—-a heavenly one. Therefore God is not ashamed to be called their God, for he has prepared a city for them.
—Hebrews 11:13–16

Sometimes before I fall asleep at night, I stop for a moment to think about heaven. I try to imagine fellowship with God free from the sinful barriers in my heart. I try to feel what it might be like to love my brothers and sisters in Christ without struggling. I think about how wonderful it will be never to be tired again, never to be hungry or rushed, pressured, impatient or in pain. I try to understand the reality of perfect peace and complete joy. And to imagine how it will feel to have Anna's arms around my neck again.

It occurs to me that God asks us to bring as much of heaven as we can to earth. We try through God's grace to fellowship with Him without barriers, to love our brothers and sisters without struggling, and to have perfect peace and complete joy. We try to bring water and plants to the desert.

God gives us courage and strength, so the water and the plants make life in the desert bearable. But we long for the lush Promised Land. No matter how green it becomes here, it is still the desert. We are aliens, foreigners. This isn't our home, and as long as we are here, we can't be completely happy. Realizing we don't belong here can be good. No wonder we are restless. No wonder we can't seem to completely fit in. And our lives can become less frustrating and less painful the more we look toward hope of heaven.

24

God *Is* Good

I am still confident of this: I will see the goodness of the Lord in the land of the living. Wait for the Lord; be strong and take heart and wait for the Lord.

—Psalm 27:13–14

Taste and see that the Lord is good; blessed is the man who takes refuge in him.

—Psalm 34:8

I have not been able to thank God for Anna's death. I have read other stories of tragedies and have heard other Christians on the radio talk about how they finally reached a place where they could thank God for the hurt. I can't do that.

I have thanked Him that she didn't have to suffer for very long, that she didn't have to go through all the painful medical procedures. I have thanked Him that the hurt somehow reawakened my dream of writing. But I just can't find it within myself to thank Him that she's gone.

In spite of that, God has somehow planted firmly in my heart the knowledge that He is good. Everything truly good that we are allowed in this life comes from Him. Somehow He takes the ugliest things in this world and miraculously, mysteriously brings good out of them.

The psalmist says, "I will see the goodness of the Lord." He does not see it now, but he is confident that he will be able to see it again during his lifetime. Then he instructs us to be strong, take heart, and wait.

You will see the goodness of the Lord again. Be strong, take heart, and wait. Then taste and see that the Lord *is* good.

25

You Won't Forget

All my longings lie open before you, O Lord;
my sighing is not hidden from you.
—Psalm 38:9

Anna had a tender heart. She often reached out to other children who were shy or lonely. In the very few weeks that she attended first grade she befriended a boy named John, who was scared about starting in big school. After Anna's death, John's mother told me how much Anna's friendship had helped him.

I pulled in the parking lot one day to pick up Caleb at middle school. Next to me was John's mother. It was his first year there, and we talked about all the big changes in his life. After she left my eyes flooded with tears. Anna would have started middle school this year. How would she have looked? What would our family have been like with this young lady around? Once again, the old familiar pain swept over me.

Sometimes I'm caught unaware, even six years after my loss. I never know when a song or a scent or a face will touch that bruised place in my heart. The pain usually subsides almost as quickly as it comes. Occasionally, however, it hangs around as a vague emptiness. But the hurt is almost reassuring now. It is a confirmation that Anna is still precious to me and that her life mattered.

Your loved one's life mattered. You won't forget how important they were. Because you remember, their life will always make a difference in your life.

26

A New Togetherness

*If an enemy were insulting me, I could
endure it; if a foe were raising himself against
me, I could hide from him. But it is you, a man
like myself, my companion, my close friend, with
whom I once enjoyed sweet fellowship as we
walked with the throng at the house of God.*
—*Psalm 55:12–14*

*Cast your cares on the Lord and He will
sustain you; He will never let the righteous fall.*
—*Psalm 55:22*

At this book's first printing, I had read and had been
told that nearly ninety percent of the couples who
lose a child will eventually divorce and eighty percent
of the parents with a handicapped child divorce. I have
since learned these statistics are exaggerated (see page
151). Still, there are tremendous pressures on families
that experience such deep pain.

Why? First, there is the grieving process. You and
the others in your family will grieve differently and on

different time schedules. If you experience a particularly difficult time simultaneously, you may be unable to reach out and comfort each other.

Second, each of you will change. It is almost like you're living with an entirely different people. You will need to get to know each "new" person, and accept and love him right where he is.

Third, for quite some time you may put your relationships on hold. You will be trying to just make it through the day. When you are surviving, there is no time or energy for nurturing. By the time the grief begins to pass, you may have forgotten the patterns of care and nurture that you had before.

When you begin to catch your breath, stop and join hands with your family. Try to travel the next part of the journey slowly and together.

27

He Will Restore Your Soul

After Job prayed for his friends, the Lord made him prosperous again and gave him twice as much as he had before. . . .

The Lord blessed the latter part of Job's life more than the first. He had fourteen thousand sheep, and he also had seven sons and three daughters. . . .

And so he died, old and full of years.
—Job 42:10, 12, 13, 17

So Boaz took Ruth and she became his wife. Then he went to her, and the Lord enabled her to conceive, and she gave birth to a son. The women said to Naomi, "Praise be to the Lord, who this day has not left you without a kinsman-redeemer. May he become famous throughout Israel! He will renew your life and sustain you in your old age. For your daughter-in-law, who loves you and who is better to you than seven sons, has given him birth."
—Ruth 4:13–15

Naomi and Job both faced tremendous loss. Naomi lost her husband and both sons. Job lost all his children, his health, and all his material wealth. He also had to deal with the ridicule of his friends.

As I look at their stories, I see several parallels. First, they were both honest with God and the people around them about their feelings. In Ruth 1:20, Naomi said, "Call me Mara," (Mara means bitter). Job said, "Even today my complaint is bitter" (Job 23:2). Second, they both recognized that the trials in their lives came from God. Naomi said, "Because the Almighty has made my life very bitter" (Ruth 1:20). Job said, "The Almighty who has made me taste the bitterness of soul" (Job 27:3). Finally, God eventually brought restoration to both of them. Naomi was provided for by a kinsman-redeemer, and she was given a grandson to continue her line. Job's wealth was restored, and he was given seven more sons and three more daughters.

In spite of their pain and bitterness, Naomi and Job maintained a relationship with God. They belonged to Him, and He held then tightly in His hand. They never deserved to be restored, but God in His abundant love brought them even more happiness than they had before.

You are God's child. He will not let go of you. Be honest about your bitterness and pain, and then let go of it. He will "restore your soul" (Ps. 23:3).

28

He Is Holding Your Right Hand

When my heart was grieved and my spirit embittered, I was senseless and ignorant; I was a brute beast before you.

Yet I am always with you; you hold me by my right hand. You guide me with your counsel, and afterward you will take me into glory. Whom have I in heaven but you? And earth has nothing I desire besides you. My flesh and my heart may fail, but God is the strength of my heart and my portion forever.

Those who are far from you will perish; you destroy all who are unfaithful to you. But as for me, it is good to be near God. I have made the sovereign Lord my refuge; I will tell of all your deeds.

—Psalm 73: 21–28

These verses are a beautiful and clear picture of the process of grieving. First, there is the initial pain and what that pain does to a person. "Senseless and ignorant" refers to the state of someone's mind who is in shock. The "brute beast" is a picture of the anger that almost always follows a loss.

Second, God leads His hurting child through the pain. He is always with you—close enough, in fact, to hold you by your right hand. He guides you with His counsel. And, most of all, He gives you the hope of heaven that sustains you when things here are unbearable. We know there will come a time of relief and joy.

At one time, I had intense anger toward the Lord. But even during that period, occasionally I'd have moments of clear thought: *I am angry at the only One who can help me. Without God I have no hope. There is only emptiness without Him.* "Whom have I in heaven but You?"

Third, a person who has gone through the grieving process and is recovering from the pain exhibits a new attitude. Once again he can say, "It is good to be near God." Here the Christian says, "I have made the sovereign Lord my refuge."

Through all the pain resulting from the loss of my dear Anna, I have learned to run to God for protection. The God who is in control of my life is always there. God is always with you, too. He is with you when you are senseless. He is close to you when you are angry. He is ready to fill you when you are empty. And He rejoices with you when once again you find that "it is good to be near God."

29

Out of the Miry Pit

I waited patiently for the Lord; he turned to me and heard my cry. He lifted me out of the slimy pit, out of the mud and mire; he set my feet on a rock and gave me a firm place to stand. He put a new song in my mouth, a hymn of praise to our God. Many will see and fear and put their trust in the Lord.

—Psalm 40:1–3

Wait patiently for the Lord. Does this mean we are to lie quietly in bed and wait for the grief to pass? Maybe God would work that way. But as I read these verses, I visualize this person floundering in the mud, crying out, "Help me! Help me, God!"

God turned and took hold of him. He pulled him out of the mud and set him down on firm ground. That person was so grateful he began to sing praises to God, right? Wrong. *God* put a new song of praise in his mouth.

My miry pit was filled with grief and pain. I couldn't pull myself out; I couldn't even reach out to God for help. But He reached down to me and lifted me out. I was unable to sing praises to God because my mouth was full of the old song—the dirge. But God put new songs of praise in my mouth again.

30

You Will Praise God Again

But I will sing of your strength, in the morning I will sing of your love; for you are my fortress, my refuge in times of trouble. O my Strength, I sing praise to you; you, O God, are my fortress, my loving God.

—Psalm 59:16–17

I have honestly shared with you some of the struggles that I went through after my daughter's death. I still don't understand many things. There were times when I didn't believe that I could sing praises again.

But today I can say, "O my Strength, I sing praise to You; You, O God, are my fortress, my loving God." Huddle in God's arms until the storm passes. You will be able to praise Him again!

3 1
My Personal Prayer

Nearly two years had passed since Anna died, and I was still angry. Night after night I prayed for God to remove the anger and bitterness from my heart.

One night God answered my prayer. I didn't hear a voice, but I knew what He was saying in my spirit. I got out of bed and wrote: "Anna's death hurt me so deeply. It was as if You ripped my heart out and crushed it under Your foot. How could that kind of hurt ever bring good? How could You love me yet hurt me like that? Am I so awful that it takes something so terribly painful to make me grow?"

And God said in my heart, "My Son died, and the pain ripped my heart out. I let Him be tortured to death, and if that weren't bad enough, I put the weight of every terrible thing in this world on His shoulders. I didn't choose my Son to bear that pain because He was so awful but instead because He was so precious to Me. And His suffering and death brought only the greatest good to the world.

"Anna's death and your suffering will bring good. You don't understand or see that good now, but if I brought so much good out of the horrible death of My Son, then believe I will bring good from the death of your daughter."

I believe You will, God. I know You will. Make me an instrument of that good.

Epilogue

Our Story

Merlin took Caleb to the florist to pick out flowers for Anna's funeral. He picked out white carnations speckled with pink and red. We asked the funeral director to keep them close to the casket throughout the graveside service. I remember looking at that little limp bouquet and wondering how Caleb would ever be able to go through the day without his best friend.

It was a sweet funeral service. We were attending Second Presbyterian Church at the time, and Paul Settle was the pastor. The church was filled with families. We had asked everyone to bring their children so they would have a chance to say good-bye. I was in shock so I don't remember much of what our pastor said, but I do remember the words "Anna's busy." He said them more than once. His words left me with a picture of Anna singing praises, playing and running to greet other children as they came into heaven.

Our home was full of people for several days. Someone was answering the phone. Someone else was feeding Daniel. My brother, Frank, spent a lot of time playing with Caleb. Someone did the laundry. Someone ironed our clothes. And for months afterwards, someone brought us supper.

I felt so far away from God. I felt so betrayed. But He used the hands and hearts of His people to love us. I will always remember the people of Second Presbyterian for that—always.

Much of the next year is a blur. Daniel was in the hospital two more times. The first time was only two weeks after Anna's death; the next time, in February, was a nine-day stay.

I remember I had a lot of kids over for Caleb to play with. He was used to playing with Anna, so it was a new experience for him to have so much time alone. For several months he pretended to be a jaguar. He crawled around the house on all fours and growled out answers to my questions. I think it was much less painful to be a jaguar than to be Caleb.

Merlin was working on his MBA. Between his school schedule and work he was able to keep his mind somewhat occupied. I spent most of my time taking care of Daniel.

We visited the grave fairly often at first. However, it wasn't too long before we decided that we needed to go separately. Merlin needed to linger there and cry over the grave. I needed to make sure there were fresh flowers and that the marker was dusted off. Then I left to do my crying elsewhere. We seemed to understand in our hearts that it was okay to grieve differently.

Sometimes people need sameness to recover from loss. The loss itself is a big enough difference. I needed change. Everywhere I looked in my little house I saw Anna.

Anna had loved raisins. For a long while, I would find little empty raisin boxes everywhere—under beds, in closets, under a bush in the backyard. Each time I would crumple into a heap of tears. A year after Anna's death, we moved. It was only a couple blocks away from our other house, but we were able to start over and there were no more raisin boxes.

But there was a huge, gaping hole in our family, and no matter how hard we tried to walk around it, we kept falling in.

The first six months I was in shock. The next six months I felt as if my heart had been ripped out. The year after that was the beginning of trying to put our family back together and trying to take some baby steps to move on.

We discovered that leukemia and Down's syndrome are somehow genetically connected. Down's children are six times more likely to develop leukemia than normal children. The doctors were concerned about Caleb and Daniel and ran several blood tests on each of them. The tests turned out fine, but the geneticist suggested that we consider not having any more children.

For many people that would be hard. For Merlin and me it was okay because we had talked about adopting a child since we were first married. Now we began seriously praying about and considering the possibility. In the summer of 1988, we began the paperwork.

In December 1989, God sent us our beautiful daughter Lydia. This adoption was as much a miracle to me as was the birth of each of my natural children. God picked out this busy little comedienne especially for our family, and He sent her to us in record time as far as adoptions go. Of course, Lydia did not fill the hole that Anna's death left in our family. She had her very own place in our family and in our hearts.

She was good for all of us, but I never anticipated how good she would be for Daniel. About a month after Lydia came, Daniel actually crawled over to me and took my hand. It was the first time ever that he sought me out. She would jump on his back and ride him like a horse, and he would giggle as hard as he could. The laughter that was so awkward at first became more natural with Lydia around.

But it was hard, too. Lydia has straight, thin, blond hair—just like Anna had. The first time I got her hair cut, she looked a lot like Anna from the back. I would catch myself anticipating Anna's chubby, round face framed under those bangs, and there would be a tug at my heart as I realized it wouldn't be till heaven that I'd see that little face again. Instead I'd find Lydia's sparkling blue eyes and impish grin. It was not that I wanted to find Anna there instead. I just wished both my daughters could be there, and I often thought about how much they would have enjoyed each other.

It has been many years since Anna went to be with her Father God. Time has passed, sometimes too slowly and at other times much too quickly. Some days tears still come. The hole in our family is still there, but we accept the empty place a lot better. We walk around it now and don't fall in quite so often.

God is big enough to take care of your grief. He is strong enough and patient enough to pull you through. Go to Him when you are hurting. He won't let you down.

One way God takes care of us is through other people. These Christians become His very hands of healing and comfort. Don't be afraid to ask your friends for help, and when things get really rough find a recommended counselor. God will provide people who want to comfort you. Look for them and let them.

I am *not* a strong person that made it through. I am a person just like you that God carried through.

> I am praying for you,
> *Robin*

Moving On:

When I share my family's story people often ask me how I'm doing now, eighteen years after Anna's death. They want to know if there are some things that I learned over time that could help them, and if I've experienced the long-term faithfulness of God. The devotions in this section are an attempt to answer some of those questions.

32

Be Vigilant and Pray

When He rose from prayer and went back to the disciples, He found them asleep, exhausted from sorrow. "Why are you sleeping?" He asked them. "Get up and pray so that you will not fall into temptation."

—Luke 22:45–46

In this passage the disciples were exhausted from sorrow—just like we are when we grieve. Christ told them to be vigilant and pray so they wouldn't fall into temptation. When you are in the middle of grieving you are, without doubt, more vulnerable to temptation. You are tired and many times your usual defenses are down. Before, I had thought that Jesus was disappointed because the disciples weren't waiting there awake praying for Him during His time of deep need. While that is probably true, it is also evident that He was concerned about *their* welfare. He was concerned that they would "fall into temptation" at a time when they were weakened by sorrow.

In the midst of your grieving listen to Jesus, stay vigilant and pray.

33

Still Hope

For in this hope we were saved. But hope that is seen is no hope at all. Who hopes for what he already has? But if we hope for what we do not yet have, we wait for it patiently. In the same way, the Spirit helps us in our weakness. We do not know what we ought to pray for, but the Spirit himself intercedes for us with groans that words cannot express.

—Romans 8:24–26

It is particularly painful for us if we're not sure the loved one we lost is a child of God. The whole point is, we *really* can't know. It is impossible to know what transpired between God and that person in those last moments or even seconds. There is still hope. For those who do not believe in eternal life, death is utterly, absolutely final. For those who don't know Christ as their savior, there is complete and irrevocable separation in death. But for those of us who know a loving, compassionate and gracious God there is the hope of the Spirit's intervention and the possibility of eternity together.

34

Warfare

For our struggle is not against flesh and blood, but against the rulers, against the authorities, against the powers of this dark world and against the spiritual forces of evil in the heavenly realms. Therefore put on the full armor of God so that when the day of evil comes, you may be able to stand your ground . . . And pray in the Spirit on all occasions with all kinds of prayers and requests. With this in mind, be alert and always keep on praying for all the saints.
—Ephesians 6:12–13a, 18

I continued to pray after we lost Anna, but I have to honestly say that it was a long time before I could understand why. Except for the fact that prayer is a way to fellowship with God, I just couldn't see what difference it made. But after I read *This Present Darkness* by Frank Peretti, I could pray again with my whole heart. I was reminded from that powerful work of fiction that prayer is not only a means of fellowship but it is also a weapon of warfare.

When I was taking Tae Kwon Do, I had to train for hours to learn to do a 360 jump or to be able to break a board. I had to practice to be able to move quickly in self-defense, to block my opponent's punch or to move in for my own. Our prayer lives are similar. It's important for us to train and practice to be able to wield this weapon of Kingdom-defense. Though God *does* want us to come to Him with our needs and He *does* care about even the tiniest things that matter to us, *prayer is not all about what we want*. It is about bringing God's kingdom here to earth, and in some miraculous way God allowing us to participate in protecting it when it comes.

35
Enough

For men are not cast off by the Lord forever.
Though He brings grief, He will show compassion,
so great is His unfailing love. For He does not
willingly bring affliction or grief to the children
of men.
—Lamentations 3:31–33

When I speak on grief I share the following story:

When the shock of Anna's death wore off, I felt like the pain would kill me and I felt betrayed by the God whose power I knew could have healed her. So I was furious. I screamed at God while I was in the shower. I screamed at Him when I was home by myself. There simply was no comforting me. One day I was actually down on the kitchen floor screaming at God and in my heart I heard Him say, "That's enough!"

Believe me, when God says, "That's enough!" you listen. It was a while before all my anger abated but I'll tell you right now, I never screamed at Him again.

Years later my daughter Lydia, then only two,

would have terrible tantrums. She'd sometimes get so out of control that nothing I did calmed her. I'd try hugging her, stroking her, singing to her, but all of my attempts to comfort her only made her angrier. Eventually I learned that the best thing to do when she "lost it" was to leave her in her room and shut the door. Her room was baby-proofed so I knew she could safely cry herself out. I'd wait listening outside her door for however long it took, hoping for the moment she'd quiet. Then I'd pick her up, rock her and whisper assurances in her ear. I know at least one time she was so upset that she got sick. That day I firmly but lovingly grasped her shoulders and said right into her face, "That's enough!"

And that day I realized that during all my screaming and crying after Anna's death God had been waiting, ready to pick me up and whisper assurances in my ear. I couldn't see Him outside the door that I had closed, but He was there listening to make sure I was safe. And I came to understand that even during those darkest of times I had continued to have a relationship with Him. I went to Him, no one else, day after day with my anger and He handled it with a deep, firm love. God is waiting for you. He is watching, keeping you safe till you cry yourself out, until there is nothing left for you but His strong arms . . . and that will be enough.

36

God *Is* Faithful

For great is His love towards us, and the faithfulness of the Lord endures forever.
—*Psalm 117:2*

We chose three hymns for Anna's funeral, "A Mighty Fortress Is Our God," "It Is Well with My Soul" and "Great Is Thy Faithfulness." The words of those hymns weren't what I felt in my heart at that time, but instead what I believed. And I have to tell you, that after all these years I have found those words reliable and true.

God *has* been faithful through the loss of my daughter, the ongoing stress of caring for Daniel, the challenges of helping Lydia through her school struggles and the numerous other trials in my life that I am unable to share here.

Every time I have been at the very end. Every time I thought I couldn't go on. Every time I wasn't sure I wanted to. God has lovingly and faithfully given me the strength to not only persevere, but also to, miraculously, find the joy.

I know if you are in the middle of the pain you can't imagine tomorrow much less eighteen years from now, but I can testify to you most assuredly, God is faithful. He *will* see you through.

37

Great Is Thy Faithfulness
Thomas O. Chisholm 1900
Wm. M. Bunyan, C. 1905

Great is thy faithfulness, O God my Father.
There is no shadow of turning with thee;
Thou changest not; thy compassions they fail not;
As thou hast been, thou forever wilt be.
Great is thy faithfulness!
Great is thy faithfulness!
Morning by morning new mercies I see;
All I have needed thy hand hath provided,
Great is thy faithfulness, Lord unto me!

To Caleb and Erin, Anna, Daniel and
Lydia—
My dreams come true.

All my longings lie open before you,
O Lord; my sighing is not hidden from
you.
Psalm 38:9

Table of Contents
Loss of a Dream

Prologue

My Story

I remember being full of dreams. What happened? Now I often find myself dragging through the day with an empty loneliness, a sense of "Is this it? Is this all there is?"

It was a long time before I understood the source of my malaise. Finally, through the Spirit's constant, gentle nudges, I realized that I was grieving. I was grieving over the loss of some of my dreams, and like grief over a death, I was experiencing denial, anger, and pain.

When you were younger, how did you picture your future? Chances are that your life is very different from what you had in mind. Life brings unexpected changes. Many times those changes set you on a completely different course. Sometimes that's a good thing. Other times the changes mean that a dream you have cherished will never come true. When this happens, there can be a terrible sense of loss.

The dream may seem insignificant, such as realizing you will never make that trip to Alaska. Or it may be life shattering, like an injury that means you will never play pro ball. But your dreams are important, no matter how small or large.

Our dreams are a part of who we are, a part of who God made us to be. When we lose a dream, we lose a part of ourselves.

While in college, I dreamed of teaching deaf children. I put all my young energy into learning sign language so I would someday be able to teach the hearing impaired. I also dreamed of being a writer. I had taken a course in children's literature and was enchanted by the more than a hundred books we were required to read. In my heart somewhere I tucked away the dream of writing a children's book.

During that time I also had some unspoken dreams. I longed to find the right man to be my husband. I thought about having children and what it might be like to be a mom. I longed for a family of my own, and I pictured that thriving, healthy family in my heart.

When I was in my second year of college, I met Merlin. I fell in love completely, though reluctantly, in an attempt to guard my heart. We were married the summer after graduation. Now, all my dreams for the future were intertwined with the dreams of this other dear person.

In our second year of marriage we moved to Greenville, South Carolina, where John Caleb was born and a year and a half later his sister Anna Elizabeth. The longing for a family of my own was being answered.

I decided to stay at home with the kids, and Merlin worked extra hard to make that possible. I had been around children all my life, but there was no way I could be ready for the reality of taking care of my own children. My experience with kids couldn't prepare me for the sudden knowledge that everything I said or did made a difference in how well this little person might do in life. Being a good mom was the hardest thing I had ever tried to do, and soon my whole being was wrapped up in it.

We enjoyed our children immensely, and after Merlin found the right job, we decided it was time to have another baby. Caleb was six and Anna was four and a half when Daniel Aaron was born.

But things were different with Daniel. At five months old he was diagnosed with Down's syndrome. All parents have dreams for their children—dreams for their future, what careers they might choose, or how many children they might have. Then there are all the little dreams—the first time they tie their shoes, read a book, learn to swim or play in a recital. And then there are the even smaller dreams—the first time they take a step or eat by themselves, learn to "go potty" or say their first word.

It soon became apparent that for Daniel the "big" dreams just wouldn't come true. And because of seizures and chronic illness many of the smaller ones wouldn't either. So we kept working toward the tiny dreams. My prayer for Daniel became simple: "Please, Lord, keep our little boy well, help him to learn to walk and feed himself and to take care of his bathroom needs." These things we took for granted with our other children, but they were huge dreams for Daniel.

When Daniel was two, our precious Anna died suddenly of unsuspected leukemia. Our hearts were broken. I remember sitting at the hospital with Merlin and saying to him, "But I was going to help her take care of her babies. She's only a little girl. She'll never know the joy of being a mama . . ."

Or the sorrow. So many of my dreams died with her.

I

God Knows Our Longings

All my longings lie open before you, O Lord;
my sighing is not hidden from you.
                                        —Psalm 38:9

Sometimes we think we know exactly what we need, but our knowledge is limited by our incomplete view of ourselves. Only God knows us completely. He is the only One who knows what is best for us, not only here on earth but also in eternity. Our deepest longings, even the ones we ourselves are not aware of, are not hidden from God. For Him our hearts are in plain view.

2

It's Okay to be Overwhelmed

> *They went to a place called Gethsemane, and Jesus said to his disciples, "Sit here while I pray." He took Peter, James and John along with him, and he began to be deeply distressed and troubled. "My soul is overwhelmed with sorrow to the point of death," he said to them. "Stay here and keep watch."*
>
> *Going a little farther, he fell to the ground and prayed that if possible the hour might pass from him. "Abba, Father," he said, "everything is possible for you. Take this cup from me. Yet not what I will, but what you will."*
>
> —Mark 14:32–36

Jesus, the perfect Son of God, was overwhelmed with what He was about to face. He knew He would be required to die a painful death, and He knew His Father could change His circumstances in a moment. He prayed for a change.

It's okay to want your circumstances to change. It is not sinful to be overwhelmed.

3

We Can't See the Whole Picture

In the same way, the Spirit helps us in our weakness. We do not know what we ought to pray, but the Spirit himself intercedes for us with groans that words cannot express. And he who searches our hearts knows the mind of the Spirit, because the Spirit intercedes for the saints in accordance with God's will.

—Romans 8:26–27

In *The Tapestry*, Edith Shaeffer compares our lives to a large, woven tapestry. The problem is we can see only the back, and often all we see there are a number of dark, messy threads. It doesn't look at all like we think it should. It's tangled and the colors are muddled. But God sees the front. He weaves the threads, light and dark together to form the beautiful, purposeful picture of our lives. Because we can't see the whole picture, when the dark patches come in our lives we despair at the ugliness. We can't see that without the contrast there would be no beauty. We don't know that even as we're in anguish God is using the losses in our lives to make the picture lovelier, more beautiful.

Our son Daniel has an immune problem so he is not able to go to school. The school system sends a teacher to our home. Staying home to care for Daniel ties me down and that has been hard for me because I love to be involved. I can't volunteer very often at Caleb's and Lydia's schools. I don't make it to the women's Bible study or the concerned parents' prayer group. But God has used this very thing to keep me still long enough to write. He took away something I desired and replaced it with a new dream, and, perhaps, a better one.

4

Life Is Frustrating

*For the creation was subjected to frustration,
not by its own choice, but by the will of the one
who subjected it, in hope that that creation itself
will be liberated from its bondage to decay and
brought into the glorious freedom of the children
of God.*

—Romans 8:20–21

"The creation was subjected to frustration."
Sometimes I feel like a fly at a window. I see the
light outside and dream about getting to it; then I buzz
full speed ahead doing my best to make it out. Instead
of finding my way, I end up crashing again and again
into the glass. The light is beautiful, and there is nothing
wrong with trying to reach it—but the truth is only God
can make the way out, and often, for our own good, He
chooses not to.

The time when the window is closed to us is a criti-
cal time. This is when God invites us to wait, rest and
trust. If we continue to fly against the glass then, when
He finally does open the window, we find ourselves too

discouraged, too afraid, or too tired to fly out. I know God has had to brush me off the sill more than once.

Maybe for you the light represents a godly mate, a steady job, a slimmer figure, or a business of your own. God doesn't promise that in this lifetime all your desires will be met. He tells us that we will be frustrated with this world, but He also promises that even in the midst of our frustrations we can find joy and "the glorious freedom of God."

5

God's Ways Are Higher

*"For my thoughts are not your thoughts,
neither are your ways my ways," declares the
Lord. "As the heavens are higher than the earth,
so are my ways higher than your ways."*
—Isaiah 55:8–9

When I read this verse I picture God walking in front of me along a mountain trail. We come to a fork. One path leads upward; it is steep and rocky and overgrown with briars. The other path leads to the right and I can tell that it would be a beautiful way to go. It appears smooth and clear and is obviously a much easier route to take. God says, "This is the way I want you to go," and He points to the difficult path up the hill. I plead with God, "Please, please let me go the other way."

But God says firmly, "No, you need to go this way. Don't worry, I'll be with you. I'll hold your hand, and if you find you can't go on, I'll carry you."

Almost two months passed between the time that Daniel was tested for Down's syndrome and when we received the results. During those two months I pleaded with God. I begged Him to let those tests come back negative, to let me take the other trail. When the doctor called us and told us the results, all I could see was the steep, rocky climb before me. At first all I noticed was how tired I was and how much I hurt. But after a time, I started to glance up and I could see things I had never seen before.

I pictured God smiling at me and saying, "Do you understand now? You would have never seen all this if I had let you take the other path."

God's plans are different—and higher—than ours.

6

Why Is There Pain?

And I heard a loud voice from the throne saying, "Now the dwelling of God is with men, and He will live with them. They will be His people, and God Himself will be with them and be their God. He will wipe every tear from their eyes. There will be no more death or mourning or crying or pain, for the old order of things has passed away."

—Revelation 21: 3–4

For God so loved the world that he gave his one and only Son, that whoever believes in him shall not perish but have eternal life. For God did not send his Son into the world to condemn the world, but to save the world through him.

—John 3:16–17

God is the ultimate recycler. In nature, everything that dies somehow contributes to new life. Leaves fall from the trees, rot, and become compost that replenishes the soil. Animals kill other animals for food. Even feces are used as a breeding place for insects or as fertilizer for plants. God wastes nothing. Neither does God waste anything that happens in our lives. He takes our most painful experiences, even the messes we make ourselves, and brings good out of them.

Why is there pain in the world? I don't believe there is a clear or simple answer to this question, but here is an attempt to explain what I understand:

Although our own pain is not always the result of our personal sin, sin, in a larger sense, is the reason pain and disease entered Eden. Sin entered the world and altered it so completely that struggle became a part of man's everyday existence (see Gen. 3).

From Genesis 3 on, the Bible's central message is redemption. It is about how God chose not to wipe us all out. It is the story of how a holy God who cannot tolerate sin made a way for us to be sinless.

Had God chosen simply to remove all the pain, He would have had to remove all the sin and therefore obliterate all the sinners. He loves us too much to give us a painless world. Instead, for now, He allows sin and pain to exist to give us time to receive the sinless nature of His Son.

He promises us that if we receive the forgiveness He has provided through Christ we will someday know a sinless, painless world. That promise gives us hope as we muddle through the hurt of our lost dreams. Like fruit trees planted in manure, we grow green and heavy with fruit because God enables us to flourish even in an odious world.

7

It's Okay to Mourn

In the land of Uz there lived a man whose name was Job. This man was blameless and upright; he feared God and shunned evil . . .

"Your sons and daughters were feasting and drinking wine at the eldest brother's house, when suddenly a mighty wind swept in from the desert and struck the four corners of the house. It collapsed on them and they are dead, and I am the only one who has escaped to tell you!"

At this, Job got up and tore his robe and shaved his head. Then he fell to the ground in worship and said: "Naked I came from my mother's womb, and naked I will depart. The Lord gave and the Lord has taken away; may the name of the Lord be praised."

—Job 1:1, 18–21

There are different ways to lose our dreams. We may realize that we will not be able to obtain something that we have longed for. We may work for years at something, then come to a dead end, or we may see a dream come true, only to have it later crumble before our eyes.

Job had a dream life. He was a good and respected man of God. He was healthy and had a fine family. He was even wealthy. Then, in just a few hours, everything was gone.

Job went into mourning. He tore at his robe and shaved his head. But even as he lay in desperate pain he recognized that God, his God, was in control.

8

Room to Grieve

*In all this, Job did not sin by charging God
with wrongdoing.*

—Job 1:22

*Yet when I hoped for good, evil came;
when I looked for light, then came darkness. The
churning inside me never stops; days of suffering
confront me.*

—Job 30:26–27

When Job's grief was new he was able to praise
God. As time passed and his great heartache
and pain continued, it became increasingly difficult for
him to praise. He began to question God. Two things are
apparent to me as I read his heart-rending prayers.

First, Job was honest with God. He simply blurted
out everything he felt. He knew God before his tragedies,
and I think he understood that God already knew what
was in his heart anyway.

Second, in spite of what appeared to be a long
silence from God, Job continued to go to God with all

his questions and complaints. Even through the pain, questioning, and turmoil, Job continued his relationship with God. God patiently listened to Job for a long time before He spoke. He gave Job room to grieve. We would do well if we could learn to give ourselves and others that same space.

9

God's Incredible Mercy

Then Job replied to the Lord: "I know that you can do all things; no plan of yours can be thwarted. [You asked,] 'Who is this that obscures My counsel without knowledge?' Surely I spoke of things I did not understand, things too wonderful for me to know.

—Job 42:1–3

Take some time today to read Job chapters 38–41.

After a time of silence, God spoke to Job. Since I've become a Christian, I've heard teaching about this book many times. Each time the focus was on Job's sin of daring to question the God of the universe. But God didn't end this book in rebuke. He ended it with restoration and mercy. When we really remember who God is—the One who marked off the earth's dimensions (Job 38:5), the One who gives orders to the morning (38:12), Who knows where the lightening is dispersed (38:24) and Whose wisdom makes the hawk take flight

(39:26)—then it becomes apparent how great His love for us must be. The fact that the Almighty God cares about our specific, personal situations is incredible!

10

Real Joy

Now is your time of grief, but I will see you again and you will rejoice, and no one will take away your joy.

—*John 16:22*

May the God of hope fill you with all joy and peace as you trust in him, so that you may overflow with hope by the power of the Holy Spirit.

—*Romans 15:13*

A dictionary defines joy as "a condition or feeling of high pleasure or delight, happiness, gladness." The Bible, however, defines joy in a more meaningful way. In scripture it is a quality of God that characterizes the life of one who believes in Him, and that will characterize the life a believer will have with Him in heaven.

In the midst of my grief and disappointment I would ask myself, "Where is the joy?" From my perspective, in the middle of the pain, I couldn't see God working.

God gave me the strength to get through those struggles one small step at a time. Each small step was a confirmation of my trust in Him. The joy I began to experience was very different from the kind of joy I had known before, but it *was* joy.

Instead of an emotional upwelling, it was a small assurance. It wasn't something I could point to and say, "See, over there, I still have joy." In fact, I'm very sure no one around me—except God—could even sense there was any joy at all. It was a tiny spark, a warm hope that kept my heart from going cold.

Christ said, "Now is your time of grief, but I will see you again and you will rejoice, and no one will take away your joy." In that one sentence He gave us permission to hurt, and then He set before us the promise of a joy that lasts forever. A joy rooted in Him and floriated with His love.

11

Moses Lost a Dream

*Therefore, you will see the land only from a
distance; you will not enter the land I am giving
to the people of Israel.*
—*Deuteronomy 32:52*

Moses spent the better part of his life working toward his dream to enter the Promised Land with his people. He faced doubts about his ability to lead. He confronted the King of Egypt. He encountered the obstacle of the Red Sea. He led a whining, unfaithful people for forty years through a desert. Then, when he was almost there, God said, "Go climb that mountain, and look at the land, but you will die before you enter" (paraphrased). Moses' dream would come to pass for his people, but never for himself.

Deuteronomy 32:51 tells us Moses wasn't allowed to enter Canaan because of his sin. God was disciplining him. Losing a dream may be the result of sin. Often, however, that isn't the case. Job was blameless and upright (Job 1:1) when tragedy hit his life.

It breaks my heart to think that after all those

years Moses wasn't allowed to achieve his dream, but I am greatly encouraged as I look at Moses' special relationship with God. God dealt with the sin in Moses' life—and that was painful—but Moses knew God face-to-face (Deut. 34:10). Imagine! Face-to-face!

12

The Ultimate Dream

I know that my Redeemer lives, and that in the end he will stand upon the earth. And after my skin has been destroyed, yet in my flesh I will see God; I myself will see him with my own eyes—I, and not another. How my heart yearns within me!

—Job 19:25–27

No matter how disappointed we become, no matter how many of our dreams are shattered, God has given us a dream that will never die—the dream of Heaven. Someday we will stand in God's presence and all the pain that sin has brought into our lives will be gone forever.

There will be days when you don't have the energy or hope to try and rebuild your earthly dreams. On those days, fix your mind and heart on the ultimate dream—Heaven.

13

God Cares

*Why do you say, O Jacob, and complain, O
Israel, "My way is hidden from the Lord; my cause
is disregarded by my God"? Do you not know?
Have you not heard? The Lord is the everlasting
God, the Creator of the ends of the earth. He will
not grow tired or weary, and his understanding
no one can fathom.*

—Isaiah 40:27–28

When you are hurting and you can't seem to find
God anywhere, it is easy to say to yourself, "God
must not care." You might even think to yourself that He
must be busy with other things. It's only natural to have
those feelings: after all, that kind of disappointment is
often what we experience in our human relationships.

But God isn't like our sinful human companions.
He is the everlasting God, the Creator. He never gets too
tired for us or too busy, and He understands our "causes"
much better then we do ourselves.

14

A Future and a Hope

*"For I know the plans I have for you," declares
the Lord, "plans to prosper you and not to harm
you, plans to give you hope and a future. Then
you will call upon me and come and pray to me,
and I will listen to you. You will seek me and find
me when you seek me with all your heart."*
—*Jeremiah 29:11–13*

Daniel is profoundly retarded. That means that
when the school psychologist tests him, his scores
are in the lowest range. He is eight years old and can't
feed himself or walk or talk. He is like a baby, only bigger.

Sometimes I look at my precious son and I feel
hopeful. He says "MaMa," and he stands alone. Maybe
he will learn enough so I can continue to care for him at
home.

Other days it's hard to keep trying. He has been
standing alone for three years, and we still haven't been
able to coax him to take his first step. He has been saying
"MaMa" for two years now, and though sometimes he

makes other sounds that can seem like words, he really has yet to use any other sounds with meaning.

I can picture the future for my other children. I can see them going off to college and then having families of their own. But I can't imagine Daniel's future. I can't come up with a plan that I feel I can live with.

But despite my limited vision, God already has a plan in place for Daniel—a plan to prosper him and not to harm him, a plan to give our family a future and a hope.

I don't know what dream you have lost. But I know very well that when some dreams are destroyed it becomes difficult to imagine a hopeful future. But God has promised us a future and a hope. We have to cling to that promise even when we can't see past today.

15

Strength Renewed

Even youths grow tired and weary, and young men stumble and fall; but those who hope in the Lord will renew their strength. They will soar on wings like eagles; they will run and not grow weary, they will walk and not be faint.
—Isaiah 40:30–31

After you grieve over the loss of your dream and then learn to accept your loss, there will come a time to start dreaming again.

You will be tired. You may be so tired that you can't think straight. There is a beautiful promise in these verses: "those who hope in the Lord will renew their strength." Place your hope for the future in God. Then get ready to fly. Not only will He give you the strength to carry on, He will enable you to soar like an eagle!

16

Seek God's Counsel

But Jehoshaphat also said to the king of
Israel, "First seek the counsel of the Lord."
—1 Kings 22:5

Y ou have moved past your hurt, and you have the
strength to dream again. Now what? Begin to look
at the world as a place full of possibilities. First, ask yourself the question: If I could do anything I wanted to do,
what would it be?

Next, write every possibility down. One by one,
bring your ideas before the Lord. Don't let your past fail-
ures or present circumstances close any of the doors that
God may desire to open for you.

God can overcome any circumstance. No matter
how incredible each idea seems, present it to God. Pray
with hope in your heart and with the willingness to relin-
quish each dream to Him.

17

Seek Others' Advice

*Plans fail for lack of counsel, but with many
advisers they succeed. A man finds joy in giving
an apt reply—and how good is a timely word!*
—Proverbs 15:22–23

You have thrown the door to your dreams wide open. Now sit down with the people who know you best, and ask them what they see as your strengths and weaknesses.

Seek counsel from your friends. They may be able to see things you can't because you are too close to your own situation to be objective. Try not to be defensive when receiving their advice, and listen with an open spirit.

Bring your ideas and the advice of your friends before the Lord and ask Him to help you sift through them.

Be aware, however, that there aren't many dreamers out there. Be careful with whom you share your heart's desires. You don't need a cold splash in the face just when you are getting the courage to jump in.

Dare to dream, seek godly human advice, and then bring it all to God so together you can throw out the rocks and polish the jewels of truth.

18

What's Most Important to You?

Yes, Lord, walking in the way of your laws,
we wait for you; your name and renown are the
desire of our hearts. My soul yearns for you in the
night; in the morning my spirit longs for you.
—Isaiah 26:8–9

What do you want most? Does your heart yearn for God in the night? Does your spirit long for Him in the morning? At night it often seems that all I yearn for is uninterrupted sleep, and in the morning, the first thing I think about is usually breakfast.

Only God can make the desire for Him first in our lives. Pray that He will fill you with a longing for His presence. He promises that if we draw near to Him our dream to be close to Him will come true.

19

Think on What Is Good

Finally, brothers, whatever is true, whatever is noble, whatever is right, whatever is pure, whatever is lovely, whatever is admirable—if anything is excellent or praiseworthy—think about such things.

—Philippians 4:8

What delights you? What are the things that give you pleasure? For the next few days notice your moments of joy and make a list of all the things that cause you gladness. Don't try to analyze what should bring you happiness. Instead, just try to notice what does.

There is so much good in every day. Often amidst the disappointments and hurt we miss the tiny joys that can help us persevere. For me, sometimes, it's as simple as how the dirt feels when I weed my pansies or the way the autumn sun stretches shadows across our backyard. It's the sweet hug my husband gives me for no special reason or my daughter's musical giggle.

Practice noticing the good that "just happens." Then begin to plan for good. Stuff as many of the things that delight you into your day as you can. Then let the joy that comes from your delight spill over onto others as you think of ways to delight them. Whatever is just, pure and good: think on *these* things.

20

Action and Faith

*Trust in the Lord and do good; dwell in the
land and enjoy safe pasture. Delight yourself in
the Lord and he will give you the desires of your
heart. Commit your way to the Lord.*
                                    —*Psalm 37:3–5*

*Lord, you establish peace for us; all that we
have accomplished you have done for us.*
                                    —*Isaiah 26:12*

In Psalm 37:3–5, each verse begins with a verb—trust,
delight, commit. We are called to participate in our
relationship with God, and yet only He can give us the
desire to do so. God wants us to dream, plan, and work,
but ultimately all that we accomplish comes from Him.

21

The Works Prepared for You

*For it is by grace you have been saved,
through faith—and this not from yourselves, it is
the gift of God—not by works, so that no one can
boast. For we are God's workmanship, created
in Christ Jesus to do good works, which God
prepared in advance for us to do.*
—Ephesians 2:8–10

Nothing we do can save us. Our very best efforts are tainted with selfishness, yet we are created to do good works. God has prepared special things for each of us to do. We are the most joyful and fulfilled when our heart's desires match up with that which God has prepared for us.

It's easy to be involved in several "good" things, and to not concentrate on God's "best." When in college, I was so excited about serving the Lord that everything looked like an opportunity. I led a Bible study, was vice president of a campus ministry, and involved in a prison ministry. I also was resident advisor, belonged to Baptist Student Union, worked with deaf children, helped handicapped students, sang in the church choir . . . and occasionally studied. None of these things was bad, but because I was trying to do them all I wasn't able to do my best at any of them.

Then I came down with mononucleosis and was on bed rest. During that time, God began teaching me that no matter how good an opportunity to serve seems, if it isn't what He has called me to do, then I shouldn't pursue it.

Ask God to show you the works that He has prepared especially for you. Then pursue them with all your heart.

22

Search Your Heart

The purposes of a man's heart are deep waters, but a man of understanding draws them out.

—Proverbs 20:5

As you look for new direction, you may discover that before you can move ahead you have to examine your heart. God knows our hearts completely, but like divers we must swim through deep waters to find the treasures hidden there.

For us, swimming around in our hearts is not natural or comfortable. Often we see dangerous and ugly things, things that scare us, but sometimes we find beautiful treasures, deposited there by God.

We have to be willing to explore the depths to be able to move on. Then bring both the good and bad to the surface where God can dispose of the ugly things and show us the light of Christ reflected in the gleaming treasures.

23

Be Confident and Persevere

So do not throw away your confidence; it
will be richly rewarded. You need to persevere
so that when you have done the will of God, you
will receive what he has promised.
                                        —Hebrews 10:35–36

God calls us to have confidence in Him and to persevere daily in our faith. When something doesn't
come easy, it doesn't always mean that it isn't what God
wants us to do. Oftentimes we reach our goals only after
lengthy toil and effort.

After twenty rejections, then three years of working with the publisher, *In This Very Hour: Loss of a Loved
One* and *Loss of a Dream* were first published in 1994.
After two years and seven rewrites my article, "Filling the
Empty Place," was published in *Guideposts*. Seven years
after I started writing professionally my first children's
book, *God Is Awesome,* was published.

In the middle of all that agonizing over every
word, working with editors, attending writing classes
and critique groups, I've got to tell you there were times

when I wanted to throw in the towel. In fact, I did lay down my pen more than once as I prayerfully wondered if God had something else for me to do. But He always brought me back to the writing. Just when I thought I was at the end I'd get a card or e-mail from someone who read my book or a "positive" rejection from an editor who took the time to tell me she liked my voice or style, and I'd be encouraged just enough to turn on my laptop and try again.

Once you see the direction God wants you to go, persevere. You might think you need confidence in yourself or your talent but all you really need is confidence in Him.

24

Balance

*He who works his land will have abundant
food, but he who chases fantasies lacks judgment.*
—Proverbs 12:11

In almost every area of our lives there is need for balance. Sometimes, the things that are seen as contradictions in Scripture are really God's way of calling us to balance in our lives.

For instance, Ephesians 2:8–9 tells us that we have been saved by grace, not works. Then in James 2:17 we are told that faith is dead without deeds. These verses seem contradictory when actually they complement each other. In Ephesians, Paul didn't say that works were not important; he said that works couldn't save us. And James didn't teach that deeds would save us; he wanted us to know that deeds are evidence of our faith.

Similarly, Proverbs 12:11 does not teach us not to dream; there are too many examples of godly dreamers in the Bible—Moses, Hannah, and Caleb are just a few. But this verse warns against chasing empty dreams.

As you surrender your dreams to God, He will give you the balance.

25

Hannah's Dream

"I prayed for this child, and the Lord has granted me what I asked of him. So now I give him to the Lord. For his whole life he will be given over to the Lord," And she worshipped the Lord there.

—1 Samuel 1:27–28

Hannah had a dream. More than anything, she wanted a son. She prayed and wept and her desire was so consuming that she became physically ill from the grief.

God answered Hannah's prayers and she was overjoyed. Then she did something amazing. She gave her answer to prayer—her heart's desire—right back to God.

She didn't just release Samuel emotionally, but she physically took him to the temple and left him there. I can't imagine the courage that took.

Before Anna died, I was probably one of the most careful moms you could have met. I was extremely careful what I ate when I was pregnant and very careful what my children ate when they grew bigger. We always buckled seat belts and wore bicycle helmets. And the kids were absolutely not allowed to watch more than an hour and a half of supervised TV a day. All this was done to help them grow up healthy and strong.

Then Daniel was born with Down's syndrome and Anna died of cancer. I had done everything humanly possible to keep them healthy, but all my best efforts were for naught.

I'm not saying that parents shouldn't try their best to watch over their children. Of course they should. But the bottom line is that our children don't really belong to us. Everything we cherish belongs to God, and we have to be willing to surrender it all to Him.

26

Caleb's Faith

*Then Caleb silenced the people before Moses
and said, "We should go up and take possession of
the land, for we can certainly do it."*
—Numbers 13:30

*But because my servant Caleb has a different
spirit and follows me wholeheartedly, I will bring
him into the land he went to, and his descendants
will inherit it.*
—Numbers 14:24

Caleb saw the same giants in Canaan the others saw. But he believed they could take the land because God was with them.

No obstacle is unconquerable when you are following God wholeheartedly. But I never feel sure I am wholehearted enough. I take many steps with far less confidence than Caleb. When obstacles loom, I wonder, is this really what God wants me to do? Had I been in Caleb's shoes, I can hear myself saying, "Maybe these giants are God's way of closing the door."

It is often difficult to know what God wants. Some things in Scripture are clear and there is no doubt, but in other areas God leaves room for His Spirit to lead each of us in different directions.

Part of faith is stepping out slowly, even when we don't feel secure in pursuit of our dreams, and then praying for Caleb's "different spirit" and the ability to follow God with our whole hearts.

27

It's Not Fair!

When morning came, there was Leah! So Jacob said to Laban, "What is this you have done to me? I served you for Rachel, didn't I? Why have you deceived me?" Laban replied, "It is not our custom here to give the younger daughter in marriage before the older one. Finish this daughter's bridal week; then we will give you the younger one also, in return for another seven years of work." And Jacob did so. He finished out the week with Leah, and then Laban gave him his daughter Rachel to be his wife.
—Genesis 29:25–28

Jacob was in love with beautiful Rachel. She was his dream wife. He worked for her seven years. But Laban deceived him and gave him Rachel's sister, Leah, instead.

Jacob could have left Padden Aran a broken man. But his love for Rachel was great, so he promised to work for Laban another seven years. Finally, he and Rachel were married.

Sometimes our efforts are thwarted, not by our own sin but by the sin of others. We want to scream, "It's not fair!" and we are right—it isn't! Somehow we have to accept this reality without giving up and push ahead with a willingness to wait for the Lord.

28

We're Aliens

All these people were still living by faith when they died. They did not receive the things promised; they only saw them and welcomed them from a distance. And they admitted that they were aliens and strangers on earth.
—Hebrews 11:13

Do you ever feel like an alien? Do you ever sit in a room full of people and think, 'Are these folks wondering which flying saucer dropped me off?'

The truth is we don't belong here. This is a foreign land, and we are on a long journey to get home. The paths available to us are the choices we each must make. As we try to move ahead we find ourselves asking, do I pick the smooth, wide road, or the rocky, narrow one? Do I follow the paths lighted by Scripture, or do I forge ahead in the dark on my own?

There are consequences to my choices. Sometimes I get lost. Sometimes the terrain is so rough that I get lost through no fault of my own. But, because I am God's child, I will complete the journey. I will make it home, and if I'll only reach for His hand, my Father will lead me there.

29

David's Dream

After the king was settled in his palace and the Lord had given him rest from all his enemies around him, he said to Nathan the prophet, "Here I am, living in a palace of cedar, while the ark of God remains in a tent."

"The Lord declares to you that the Lord Himself will establish a house for you: When your days are over and you rest with your fathers, I will raise up your offspring to succeed you, who will come from your own body, and I will establish his kingdom. He is the one who will build a house for my Name, and I will establish the throne of his kingdom forever."

—2 Samuel 7:1–2, 11–13

David had a dream. He wanted to build a "house" for God. It was a wonderful dream, but God had a different plan. David sought the counsel of Nathan, and through him God revealed that David's descendents would fulfill the dream. But in *God's* plan, the "house" would actually be a lineage and out of that lineage would come the Savior of the world.

When I was twenty-seven, I had the opportunity to spend a week with my birth father. It was the first time I had seen him in several years and probably only the fourth time since my parents' divorce when I was four. During that week I was able to share the gospel with him. Three months later he was diagnosed with terminal cancer. We corresponded over the next months, and when he no longer had the strength to read, I sent him Bible tapes to listen to. I believe he received Christ before his death.

His mother—my grandmother—was a Christian. I know from my conversations with him that she spent a lot of time in prayer for her son. She died when he was a very young man, but I believe her prayers reached across the generations to my heart and then to his. Though she didn't see it, her life made a difference.

As we reach for goals in this lifetime, we have to remember that what we do here doesn't always end when we are gone. Our lives have purpose in God's plan for the future, and some of our dreams may be fulfilled when we are not here to see them.

30

The Most Extraordinary Dream

However, as it is written: "No eye has seen,
no ear had heard, no mind has conceived what
God has prepared for those who love him."
—1 Corinthians 2:9

Try, for a moment, to imagine your life filled with every good thing, with every dream fulfilled. Now, with that picture in mind, try to understand that what God has prepared for you in heaven is far more wonderful than what you are able to envision.

Heaven is the most marvelous hope, the most extraordinary dream, and the God of the universe has promised His children that it will come true!

3 1

My Prayer for You

May the God of hope fill you with all joy and peace as you trust in him, so that you may overflow with hope by the power of the Holy Spirit.

—Romans 15:13

This verse is my prayer for you. My prayer for each of you who have lost a dream is that you will find new hope in God.

New hope doesn't take away the pain. Some losses will always sadden our hearts. But hope for the future gives us the strength to continue on, to run the race, to persevere. It gives us the ability to complete the journey even if we have to carry a load of pain to the end. Hope in God guarantees we will not have to carry the burden alone and that one day it will be lifted from us, forever.

Epilogue

New Dreams

During summers between college terms I worked at the elementary school in my hometown. One summer I became great friends with a girl I worked with named Beverly. We claimed to be sisters since both our last names were Prince, and we enjoyed the confusion that caused since she was black and I was white.

One day she walked in looking sad. I asked her what was wrong and she said, "Robin, I'm just going through changes." I had never heard that expression before but have since come to appreciate it as an appropriate and vivid way to describe the ups and downs in our lives.

We all go through changes. I never ended up teaching deaf children as I had planned. With a handicapped child my family was very different from my earlier dreams. Being a mom was harder than I ever imagined. All of these things were changes and took some adjustment of expectations.

With some of the changes in our lives there is only a moment's hesitation, like hitting a pothole in the road. With others it seems as if the road ends at a great chasm and there is no way to move on and get past the terrible emptiness. But God's grace is big enough to reach across even the deepest of pits, and in two ways He began to reach over and help me rebuild a bridge of dreams.

First, one day, about two years after Anna died, as I drove home from Daniel's physical therapy I began to pray. We had applied for adoption and had been waiting over a year. That is a short time as far as adoptions go, but Caleb was already ten and we really hoped our baby would come before he grew too much older. That day I asked God to please send our baby daughter soon. And in my heart I heard Him say, "I'll send your baby after you write this book for Me."

I had been thinking about writing a devotional for people who are grieving. While I was in the middle of all my hurt, I marked all the verses in my Bible that brought me comfort and they weren't the usual verses that people quote in difficult times. I thought these different verses might help others in pain, but I hadn't yet started writing.

As soon as I got home that day I began. I wrote for three days straight, and then spent a couple of weeks reviewing and adding to it. Our daughter, Lydia Grace, was born about the time I finished the book, though she didn't come to live with us until a month later.

Several months after that, I had lunch with our pastor's wife and told her about the book. She read it and encouraged me to send it out. That was the beginning of my writing.

I arranged a babysitter one or two days a week and went to the library to write. I started to crave the time I could spend writing. Before long I realized that being a writer had been a dream of mine for many years. Somehow, along the way it had been forgotten.

One day when my oldest son, Caleb, and I were looking through my old scrapbooks I found my first rejection letter: when I was nine years old I had sent a poem to *Reader's Digest*. I also found a seventh grade newspaper with several articles that I had written and a high school magazine that had published a couple of my poems.

In all the busyness of being a wife and mother and then in all the pain, I had lost who I was. I had completely forgotten my dream of writing children's books. I had forgotten that I liked unusual clothes and bright colors, and I had forgotten what a crazy sense of humor I had. Slowly, God brought all of these things back into my life and with my personal growth came healing.

The second thing that happened was that I began to really appreciate the special family God had given me. Each of my precious children has very special needs, and there are days when their needs overwhelm me. But along with their specialness comes unspeakable joy.

Caleb took the SAT in the seventh grade for the Talent Identification Program at Duke University. His scores were very high, and we were invited to Duke for a special weekend recognition ceremony and conference. At the conference, the speakers talked about the special needs of gifted children and how as parents we have to make sure they have enough challenges to be happy.

Instead of my challenging Caleb, he has always challenged me. He accepted Christ at a very young age, and from the time he was about four asked me questions like, "If God is love, then does that mean He loves Satan?"

Living with Daniel is like living with an angel. I know it is theologically impossible, but I have never seen any sin in his little life. He just wants to love and be loved. There is a sweetness in him that is unexplainable.

When Lydia was two and a half she was diagnosed with ADHD (Attention Deficit and Hyperactivity Disorder). In Lydia's busyness there is an enthusiasm for life that is contagious. To walk to our house from the car we have to pass a rose bush. Lydia always stops to smell the fragrant pink blossoms, and she won't let me go in until I smell them too. She delights in a bubble bath and refuses to get out till every bubble is gone. She adores eating spaghetti and experiences it so thoroughly that it takes me an hour to get all the sticky noodles off her and the surrounding furniture. With Lydia around I won't miss anything. She makes sure I pay attention to the everyday joys.

I pray that if you are feeling trapped and hopeless in the loss of your dreams, God will somehow use this devotional to light the tiny spark of hope that will get you going. Take some time to rest and heal in the comfort of His loving arms, then get ready because God has a new dream for you—a new future—a new hope.

My life is very different from what I dreamed. But it is what God has chosen for me. It is God's dream for me, and I am trusting that it is better than what I imagined.

Moving On

Daniel is twenty years old now. He is like a young toddler—just bigger. He is one of the happiest and most delightful people I know.

Lydia is sixteen. She struggled so long and hard with school that finally in the seventh grade I started homeschooling her. The one-on-one attention seems to be what she needs. She loves singing, is a talented artist, and is fascinated with animals. She plans, one day, to become a cosmetologist.

Caleb, now twenty-six, is married to a terrific young lady named Erin and is living in Los Angeles. He is a screenwriter's assistant, and soon, I am confident, will be a screenwriter. His comic book, *Redchapel,* will be published in 2006.

Merlin is the smartest man I know, a wonderful father and my best friend. He works as a manager at a local manufacturing company, and plays golf if he gets the chance. I work part time for my brother as a business consultant, homeschool Lydia, and when I can squish it in, I write.

And our dream is to live somewhere, not too far from the beach, where we can finally slow down a bit.

We don't want a large house. But we dream of having an extra room where every so often other couples with special-needs children can come for a weekend away to rest and recreate and rekindle their love.

32

Take Pause

Jesus looked at them and said, "With man this is impossible, but not with God; all things are possible with God.
—Mark 10:27

"Everything is permissible"—but not everything is beneficial. "Everything is permissible"—but not everything is constructive.
—I Corinthians 10:23

The last six years I have spent time studying and then teaching the Creative Problem Solving Technique. This technique has specific steps that lead you eventually to an action plan that will, at least in part, solve the problem you start with. But the most important principle of the technique is setting aside your judgment long enough to come up with long lists of facts, then ideas.

As we look ahead to new dreams and begin to explore our options, it is easy to instantly judge what God brings to our mind as impossible or silly before we give the thoughts a chance. It would have been easy for

Noah to decide right away that building a boat in the desert was silly. Caleb could have been sensible and not tried to fight an army of giants. And, remember, Moses got in trouble for immediately and firmly deciding that it would be impossible for him to speak for God.

As you search for a new beginning, take time to write a long list of possibilities for your future. Don't stop to evaluate or judge anything as you write. Open your heart to even the most unusual and ridiculous thoughts. Then set the list aside. Don't pick it up till the next day, or even the next week. Then prayerfully, with God's direction, begin evaluating what you've written. You may be surprised where He leads you when you are genuinely open to His Spirit. You might even find yourself building a boat in the desert!

33

The Next Thing

*Let us not become weary in doing good, for
at the proper time we will reap a harvest if we do
not give up.*
                                    —*Galatians 6:9*

*I can do everything through Him who gives
me strength.*
                                    —*Philippians 4:13*

Daniel still wears diapers. We still have to feed him.
He is still completely dependent on us for his
care. But he can walk now if we hold his hand. He can
say "Bye, Bye," "Eat," the names of everyone in his family,
and one Easter he actually said "Amen!"

Once someone asked me if I was concerned about
Daniel's quality of life. I answered truthfully that Daniel
is the happiest person I know. He wakes up in the morning to hugs and kisses. He is tenderly fed and bathed, then
he has school, which consists of therapy and practice. He
plays for the rest of the day. Occasionally he goes for a
ride or gets to go to Camp Grandma where he devours

homemade mashed potatoes and lots of attention. He laughs and smiles most of his waking hours. Then he goes to bed with more hugs and kisses and dreams about stuff I can't begin to imagine.

When Daniel was around ten years old I found myself completely exhausted, spent. Ten years of taking care of a baby will do that to a person. I cried out to God for help and He sent us Phyllis, Daniel's caregiver. Provided by a state program, Phyllis comes five days a week. She feeds Daniel, baths him and keeps him company while I work part time, write and homeschool Lydia. Phyllis has become one of my dearest friends and part of our family. She is an answer to prayer and one way that God is taking care of me.

I still don't know what the future holds for Daniel, and there are times when I get very tired. All I know to do is the next thing, and then the next. I just can't look too far ahead. But I take comfort in knowing that God sees what is ahead for us, He knows my needs and Daniel's, and I am learning to leave them all in His hands.

Gather your fears for your future and place them firmly in your Father's hands. I know you are weary, but He will give you the strength to do the next thing.

34

For Caregivers

"Then the righteous will answer him, 'Lord, when did we see you hungry and feed you, or thirsty and give you something to drink?'
"The King will reply, 'I tell you the truth, whatever you did for one of the least of these brothers of mine, you did for me.'"
—Matthew 25:37, 40

You know what? I still don't make it to those Bible studies. Only rarely can I take supper to a friend in need or visit an elderly neighbor. I had believed that by now I'd be able to reach out more. And I'm often frustrated as I see needs and find myself unable to help.

When you are going through a long illness with a family member, or one of you children is chronically ill, you may find that you have little time or energy to reach out like you want to. And if this care-giving lasts for years, as it has for me, you may start to feel guilty about your lack of involvement.

The truth is, the care-giving itself may take all your energy. You may not be able to do even one more thing.

But remember, when God chose this family for you He set before you a ministry. As you are feeding, diapering and hugging your loved one you are feeding, diapering and hugging Christ. To take care of someone who is helpless is a tender and noble calling . . . a calling that leads to eternal life. (Matthew 25:46b)

35
Two Are Better

*Two are better than one, because they have
a good return for their work: If one falls down,
his friend can help him up. But pity the man who
falls and has no one to help him up! . . . A cord of
three strands is not quickly broken.*
—*Ecclesiastes 4:9–10, 12b*

My husband, Merlin, and I will be married 29 years this summer. In spite of the pain of losing a child and the pressures of raising three special needs children, God has enabled us to maintain a sweet and close relationship. There have been some challenging times for us. We have both been in and out of states of exhaustion, discouragement and depression. But we have been blessed with a love that we can count on in one another.

People ask us how we made it through the tough times together. I know that it is only by the grace of God, and not short of a miracle, that we are still married and very much in love. But there are a few things that we have done that I think have helped.

First, we haven't taken our love or marriage for

granted. We know all earthly relationships are fragile. So even during the most challenging times with our children we have taken time to be alone together. There were times when we were fortunate enough to be able to go out once a week. Other times when the demands of our family were particularly pressing we might only work out a "date" once a month. At least once a year we try to take a weekend away. This requires a lot of planning and effort. And leaving children behind can be especially hard for moms who have lost a child. But we know that besides our children's heritage in the Lord, the most important thing we can give them is a loving, stable family. The time away is not only for us. It is also for them.

Secondly, we have allowed each other the freedom to recreate. It can be tempting when dealing with extraordinary demands at home to pull at each other constantly. Merlin and I have been able to work out ways to take turns so that each of us has a little time to fill ourselves back up. For Merlin, over the years that has been softball, tennis or golf. For me it was art classes, Tae Kwon Do or weekends away with friends. Neither of us has the time or energy to do too much so we carefully choose one thing at a time. But having a place to "fill up" enables us to have something left to give one another.

And third, we have an amazing support group. Both our moms have been willing, over the years, to keep the kids so we can have some time away. I know I can depend on Daniel's caregiver, Phyllis, to occasionally take up the slack. And I count on my sweet friends, Nancy, Pam, Marie, Patty, Ellen, Darla, Jann and others for their listening ears and fervent prayers.

Note: When I first wrote these devotions in 1990 I read in more than one source that couples who have lost a child have a ninety percent chance of divorcing. I have since learned from the Compassionate Friends organization that the divorce rate of grieving families is not as high as then believed, and that tragedy sometimes brings spouses closer together.

36

He'll Make a Way

"When did we see you sick or in prison and go to visit you?"

—*Matthew 25:39*

O ne day when I was feeling particularly isolated, wondering if my life was making a difference, I came across this Scripture and I prayed: "Lord, how can I go visit prisoners when most days it is difficult for me to leave my house?"

The mail came just as I finished praying. Now, being a very optimistic writer I usually dash to the mailbox when I hear the mail truck's brakes down the road. Because, you see, one of those envelopes might contain the letter that says that some smart editor has finally deemed one of my manuscripts publishable. So I made my usual mail dash and found instead an envelope from the Coconino County Sheriff's office. Inside was a letter from the chaplain there explaining how he uses *Loss of a Loved One* in his ministry to prisoners. It was hard to leave my house, but God had made a way for me to visit prisoners—in Arizona!

If reaching out in the conventional ways proves difficult in your situation look for other ways to serve. One thing that you can do, no matter what your situation, is to pray. Most churches have a prayer request line or e-mail. Get on the list, print it out and post it somewhere where it is easy to see. Then pray. In spare moments between tasks, lift the people around you up in prayer. You will be ministering to them, and praying will also help you remember how blessed you are.

Other ways to serve from your home are:
1. Phone people you know who are lonely. Get a headset for your phone so you can work as you talk.
2. Send cards or e-mails.
3. Start a newsletter for people experiencing challenges like yours.
4. Pray for and encourage missionaries.
5. Start a blog or web site to encourage others.

There are many possibilities. Brainstorm a list. Then pray, asking God to show you where and when to start.

It may be tomorrow, or years from now, but one day, when you are ready, God will tug at your heart and give you a new vision for ministry—a new dream. In the meantime, take care of yourself physically, mentally, emotionally and spiritually so you'll be ready when He calls.

37
A Challenge

*I pray also that the eyes of your heart may be
enlightened in order that you may know the hope
to which he has called you, the riches of his glorious
inheritance in the saints, and his incomparably
great power for us who believe. That power is
like the working of his mighty strength which he
exerted in Christ when he raised him from the
dead . . .*

—Ephesians 1:18–20a

Reading this book may stir up questions about your
faith. According to scripture there are three kinds
of people: Those who have never heard the gospel; those
who have heard and have done nothing about it; and
those who have heard the gospel, accepted it as truth,
and understand that it is the most important thing in
their lives.

Those of you who have never heard or who have
heard but don't understand what knowing Christ as your
personal savior means, I challenge you to ask God to
show Himself to you, then pick up a Bible and read daily

in the book of John.

Those of you who have heard and believe there is a God and that Jesus is His son but that knowledge doesn't affect the way you live—you don't feel you have a personal, growing relationship with Him—I challenge you to ask Jesus to be the Lord of your life. That means to ask him to be the one in control, not you. Then pick up a Bible and read daily in the book of Romans.

And those of you who know Jesus as your personal savior . . . He *is* the most important thing in your life, but your world has been turned upside down by death, illness or some other tremendous trial and you don't know where He is right now: I challenge you to go to Him with your questions and pain. Talk to Him honestly about your doubt, then pick up your Bible and read daily in the book of Psalms.

Please visit my web site at
www.RobinPrinceMonroe.com
or e-mail me at
WordsThatBless@aol.com.

I would love to hear from you.

May he give you the desire of your heart
and make all your plans succeed.
We will shout for joy when you are victorious
and will lift up our banners in
the name of our God.
May the Lord grant all your requests.
—Psalm 20:4–5

Blessings,
Robin

Contact Robin Prince Monroe
or order more copies of this book at

TATE PUBLISHING, LLC

127 East Trade Center Terrace
Mustang, Oklahoma 73064

(888) 361 - 9473

Tate Publishing, LLC

www.tatepublishing.com